BATMAN IN
The Black Egg of Atlantis

Neal Barrett, Jr.

Illustrated by Sal Amendola

Little, Brown and Company
Boston   Toronto   London

For all my old pals in the neighborhood, way back when. If you borrowed any of my comic books, I *still* want them back.

— Neal Barrett, Jr.

First Edition

ISBN 0-316-17768-7
Library of Congress Catalog Card Number 92-56757
Library of Congress Cataloging-in-Publication information is available.

10 9 8 7 6 5 4 3 2 1

BUF

Published simultaneously in Canada by Little, Brown & Company (Canada) Limited

Printed in the United States of America

CHAPTER 1

"Time to Die, Batman!"

The cold wind howled through the dark, empty heights of Gotham City, stung the tall towers, then swept like a chill and cutting blade to the shadowy streets below. Rookie officer Bobby Meaders shivered and ducked his head deeper into the collar of his coat, but the heavy jacket failed to keep the wind from slicing clear through to the bone.

Bobby Meaders hated the cold, but he hated the wind even more. In the early-morning darkness, it sounded like the howl of ghostly wolves. He imagined their gray and hulking shapes padding toward him through the night. He imagined he could hear their hot breath, see their red eyes glowing with an unearthly light.

Something scraped against the wet streets. Bobby turned quickly, his hair climbing the back of his neck. He shined his flash into the dark alleyway to his right. Fog rolled in from the nearby waterfront, choking off the beam of light.

The alley was empty. Bobby forced a laugh, snapped off the flash, and continued on his way.

"You've got the shakes, pal," he told himself. "There is nothing out there but cats and stray dogs, and they're a lot colder than you."

Still, he found himself looking back over his shoulder and walking a little faster down the street. Nothing was there, Bobby knew, but it isn't that easy to toss your fears aside when the sounds come at you in the night.

Not for the first time, Bobby Meaders wished he hadn't talked back to Sergeant Mike "Bulldog" O'Brien. O'Brien had been on his back for a week, and it seemed like the right thing to do at the time. Now, with his feet half frozen and his ears cold enough to drop off, he could see it was a foolish thing to do. Even top officers on the force stayed out of O'Brien's way. O'Brien had ice-water eyes that said, "Hands off, mister — I eat captains for lunch."

A rookie cop with four months on the force got more than a pair of cold eyes. What he got was the "graveyard beat," walking the chill October streets from midnight to six. Old hands told Bobby he was lucky, that O'Brien had let him off light. "Bulldog" had handled rookies for twenty years, and he had a lot *worse* tricks up his sleeves.

Maybe it was true, Bobby thought, but if this was one of O'Brien's *easy* punishments, he didn't want to hear about the rest.

Far down the block, tires hissed on the street. Headlights shone dimly through the fog, like the eyes of some creature undersea. The car turned, and the lights winked away.

2

Bobby stopped as the big clock atop City Hall began to toll dully in the night. The clock was a pale yellow moon, barely visible through the mist.

Three o'clock. It wasn't Bobby's favorite time. It wasn't even close. Three was a dread gray hour that belonged to both the day and the night. People still awake at this time sat alone and faced their worst fears. Those who were asleep wished they weren't, for they were caught in a web of awful dreams.

Bobby turned the corner that led to the front of City Hall. Halos of light circled the streetlamps by the curb, but the plaza that faced City Hall was empty and black.

No . . . pitch-black, but not empty at all. . . . There was something, something out there that didn't quite belong. . . .

Bobby stopped, took a deep breath, and held it. He walked a few steps off the curb and stopped again. The swirling clouds of fog played tricks on his eyes. It was there, then just as quickly gone. Something dark, something squat and square, *there,* and then swallowed in the fog.

Bobby moved closer. He had his jacket unbuttoned, his hand on the butt of the service revolver strapped to his side. He left his flash alone. The light was next to useless in the fog.

The mist rolled and twisted, as if it had a life of its own. Bobby paused. *There!* The black shape appeared again. He took two steps through the fog, then three. The dark thing was right there, looming above him, not twenty feet away.

Bobby stopped, suddenly frozen in his tracks. There was one big square, maybe seven feet high. And on top of the square, there was another, smaller shape. The smaller shape looked familiar. Bobby was certain he had seen it somewhere, but he couldn't remember where. . . .

And in that moment, the writhing fog parted, and Bobby saw the thing clearly for the first time.

Bobby Meaders stumbled back, a cry stuck in his throat. Now he could see the raised platform draped in black cloth. Black urns filled with thorny plants and withered leaves lined the top of the platform. Now Bobby knew why the shape atop the platform looked familiar. He had seen that shape many times before. It was a black metal casket, gleaming in the dim half-light. A dark, wilted wreath rested on the casket like a coiled and deadly snake. The lid of the casket was open to the night. If there was anything *inside* that casket, Bobby couldn't see it from the street, and he certainly didn't want to find out.

Bobby Meaders turned and ran across the plaza through the night. He ran and he didn't look back. He was sure that if he did, he would see something black and enormous on his heels, something far more deadly than the red-eyed wolves he'd imagined in his head.

His cap fell off along the way, and Bobby didn't stop to pick it up. "Bulldog" O'Brien could scream at him if he liked. Bobby wasn't going back *there*. . . .

Just outside Gotham City, Bruce Wayne awoke with a start. He sat up quickly, drew in a breath, and stared across the darkened room. For a moment, the nightmare that had jerked him out of sleep clung to him like a second skin. His face and chest were beaded with cold droplets of sweat.

4

Bruce Wayne had known fear before. As Batman, he had faced it a thousand times in Gotham City's dark streets and high towers. Usually, though, the enemies he had faced had been real — The Joker, Catwoman, Clayface. The thing that had chased him across the chill plains of his nightmare was something else again. It had no face, and it had no name. It was simply *there*, a pure and deadly evil, a cold and unnatural force. . . .

Wayne turned as light poured in from the hall. Alfred peered around the door, then stepped into the room.

"Is everything all right, Master Bruce?" Alfred said. "I thought I heard you call out."

"It was nothing," Wayne said. "I had a bad dream." He put his feet on the floor and yawned. "What time is it, Alfred? It must be the middle of the night."

"Not quite, sir," Alfred said. "It's a quarter to four."

"*Four?*" Wayne moaned and rubbed a hand across his face. "I'm going back to bed, Alfred. Give me a call about seven, if you would."

Alfred didn't move from the foot of the bed. "I'm afraid not, sir."

Wayne looked at his butler and longtime friend. He didn't have to ask why he would not be getting any sleep. He knew Alfred well, and he could read the message clearly in his eyes.

"Trouble, right?" said Wayne.

"Yes, sir," Alfred said. "The usual kind, I'm afraid." He moved across the room and pulled the heavy drapes aside. Wayne stood and walked to the window. A chill rain peppered against the glass. A thick fog covered the dark horizon. Still, the powerful beam of the Bat-Signal sliced through the gloom to leave the circular image of a bat on the low-hanging clouds. The Bat-Signal told Wayne that Police Commissioner James Gordon needed Batman in Gotham City.

"You would think, sir," Alfred said with a sigh, "that just once the wrongdoers of Gotham could commit a crime during some decent hour of the day."

Wayne shook his head. "Vermin don't care for the light, Alfred. They much prefer the night."

But the night doesn't belong to them alone, he thought. *It also belongs to me. . . .*

The rain had settled down to a light, chilling mist by the time Batman arrived at City Hall. He left the Batmobile outside the yellow "crime scene" tapes and walked toward the broad plaza. Red and blue lights blinked atop a dozen police cars. Uniformed officers and plainclothes detectives swarmed over the area like an angry tribe of ants. The center of their attention was a black platform in the middle of the plaza. Resting atop the platform was an object that Batman recognized at once. It was an open black coffin with a black wreath resting on its lid.

Batman paused. A sudden, unfamiliar chill touched the back of his neck. He didn't have to ask why. There was something dreadfully familiar about the scene before him now. He knew he hadn't seen it in his dream. In the dream, there was nothing but the dread and awful plain, and the nameless thing that chased him through the hellish night.

But it was there, Batman thought. *I couldn't see it, but I know the black coffin was there. . . .*

"Batman, I'm glad you're here."

Batman put his thoughts aside as the tall, lanky figure of Police Commissioner Gordon stalked toward him across the plaza.

"What have we got here, Jim?" Batman asked his old friend.

Gordon reached out and gripped Batman's hand. The commissioner hadn't stopped to shave. The silver hair at his temples looked frazzled, and his eyes behind the thick-lensed glasses were red from lack of sleep.

"A young officer named Bobby Meaders stumbled on it," Gordon explained. "A little after three. It scared him pretty bad. I don't guess I blame him for that."

"It's not a sight you'd care to run into in the dark," Batman said.

Gordon touched Batman's arm and walked him toward the dark platform. "So far, we've been leaving it to the lab boys," he said. "Getting some pictures, checking the thing out. The bomb squad's on the way. They'll bring some dogs to sniff the place out."

Batman nodded. "Someone's having a lot of fun." He peered over his shoulder into the dark. "Probably watching us right now."

"They're not going to have any *fun* when I get my hands on them." Gordon gave Batman a grim look. "I've got a police force to run. I don't have time for any —"

The commissioner's words were lost as one of the

policemen let out a startled cry. A sharp, whistling sound pierced the air. Darkness seemed to explode from the open coffin. Officers raced for cover as a cloud of black dust spewed into the air, followed by a fountain of cold water. In seconds, a black and dirty rain descended on the startled policemen. Gordon and Batman stared, as a flock of black crows and ravens burst from the casket, shrieking and squawking, nipping angrily at everyone in sight before they disappeared.

As the dark rain began to vanish, a black umbrella suddenly sprang up from the coffin in a cloud of black smoke. Batman felt his throat tighten. He left Gordon's side and leapt for the platform. Gordon called after him, warning Batman that there might be further danger still. Batman didn't answer. He had already spotted the sign hanging from the dark umbrella.

The sign was printed in a neat, spidery script:

Citizens of Gotham City:
You are cordially invited to attend the FUNERAL
of BATMAN, at midnight, Saturday, October 31,
Halloween night. Come one, Come all!
                              The Penguin

"What is it," Gordon called from below, "what does it say?"

Batman showed Gordon a grim smile. "It seems to be an invitation to a party. Now I've got somewhere to go on Halloween. . . ."

CHAPTER 2

"As Old as Evil Itself . . ."

Officers from the Gotham City crime lab and the bomb squad scrambled over the platform and peered into the empty coffin. Batman watched from the street. He knew what they were looking for — evidence that might tell them where the platform, the black powder, and the coffin itself were purchased. He was sure they would find very little that would help. His old enemy, The Penguin, was much too clever to leave an easy trail for the law.

"I guess I shouldn't be surprised he's back," said Commissioner Gordon. "It's too much to hope that he'd simply disappear after his last crime spree."

Batman shook his head. The early-morning fog had vanished with the first hint of dawn, but the chill of the night was still there. Autumn usually brought lazy, pleasant days to Gotham City, but this year winter seemed eager to rush in and have its way.

"The Penguin will give up crime about the same time you take up ice skating, Commissioner," said Batman.

"I'd be glad to start," Gordon said wearily, "if you think that would help." He reached up, removed his glasses, and squinted at the towers of Gotham City.

"I'm sure we're thinking the same thing," he said. "It's pretty obvious, isn't it? Midnight on Halloween. The date of your, ah, *funeral* is the same night as the opening of the museum. The night the Black Egg of Atlantis goes on display to the public."

"Exactly," said Batman. "The Penguin is obsessed with birds — or anything to *do* with birds. He can't help himself. And if something of great value comes along, something *connected* with birds . . ."

"Like the Black Egg. I personally supervised its delivery this week," Gordon finished. "Batman, The Penguin would give his right arm to own something like that!"

His arm or mine, thought Batman. . . .

The Penguin had been on Batman's mind for some time, long before that morning. The master criminal had dropped out of sight after his last run-in with Batman and the law, but he had disappeared before. It was foolish to imagine that he wouldn't return again.

And, as Gordon said, the Black Egg was a perfect target for The Penguin. At midnight on October 31, all the "important people" in Gotham City would be on hand for the grand opening of the Thomas and Martha Wayne Memorial Museum. It was a project funded by multimillionaire Bruce Wayne, through the Wayne Foundation, in memory of his parents. The highlight of the evening would be the unveiling

11

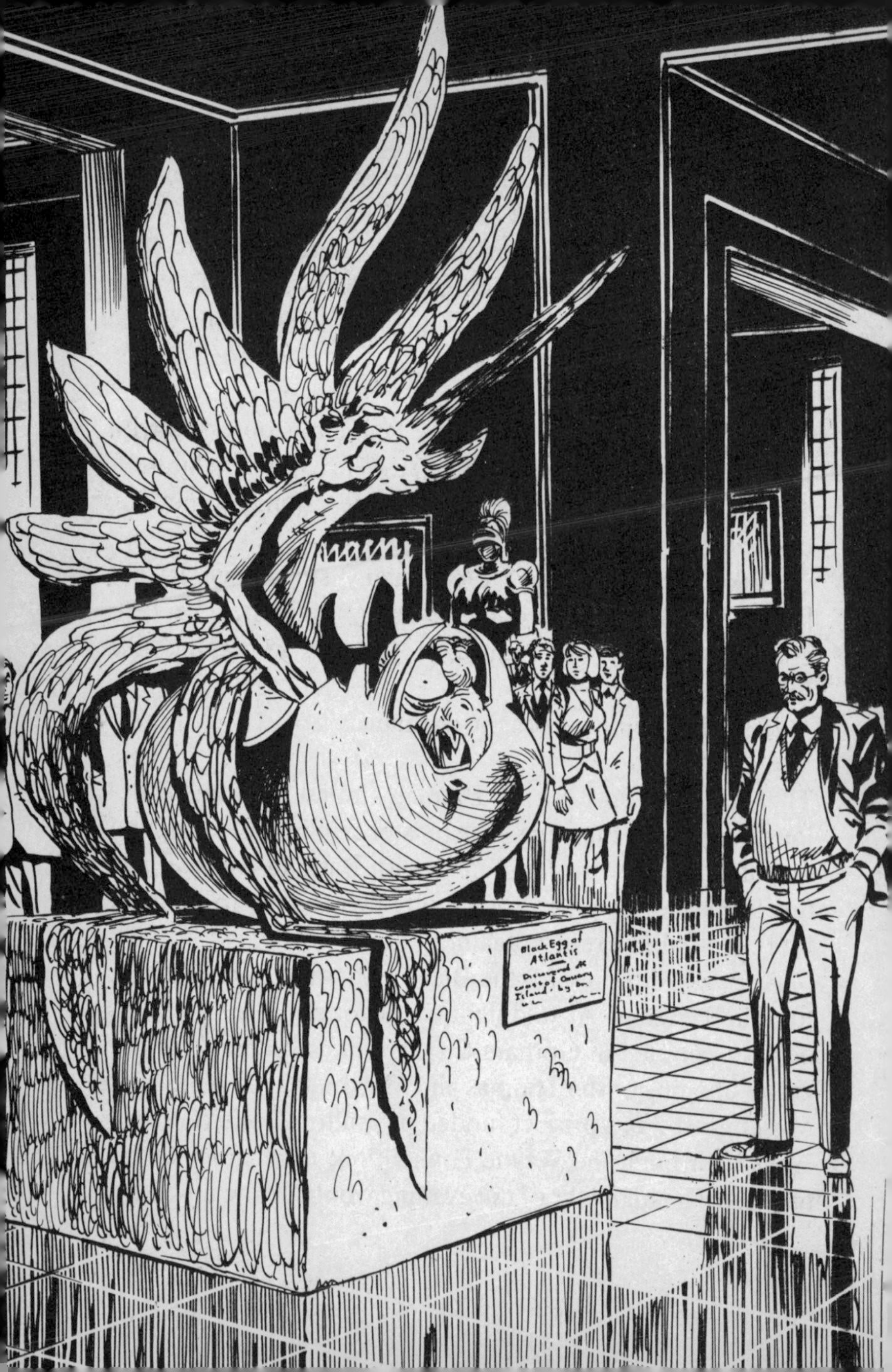

Black Egg of
Atlantis

of the Black Egg of Atlantis, one of the most important archaeological finds of the century.

The Black Egg had been discovered by Dr. Amelia Torn in the deep waters off the Canary Islands. Dr. Torn claimed the two-ton stone carving came from the ruins of the lost continent of Atlantis. Many scientific experts questioned the Black Egg's origin. Still, whether it actually came from Atlantis or not, the Black Egg was a sensational find, and its unveiling had excited both the public and the news media alike. Everyone was anxious to get a look at the strange statue that had experts arguing all over the world.

Standing with Commissioner Gordon in the dreary morning light, Batman suddenly felt uneasy about the opening Saturday night. As Bruce Wayne, he had given the museum to Gotham City, and he was one of the few people who had actually seen the Black Egg. If the public was expecting some "ordinary" relic of the past, they were in for a surprise. The Black Egg was a hideous thing to see. It was the image of a bird-god hatching from its egg. It tore at its shell with a cruel, hooked beak and savage claws. One terrible eye peered from the egg, and in that eye Batman had seen a look of hate and madness as old as evil itself. The bird-god seemed to say, *I am here, and I bring with me a hunger that you have never dreamed of before. . . .*"

Bruce Wayne had wondered at the time what kind of people had created this awful thing. What terrible rites had they performed in its honor? Seeing the Black Egg in the present was enough. It was hard to imagine what had happened in the dark and distant past.

*   *   *

"What? What's that, Jim?" Batman brought himself back from his thoughts as he heard the commissioner speak.

"I said we shouldn't be surprised at The Penguin's little display," Gordon said. "It's just the way he thinks. He can't just *steal* something like a common criminal. He has to let us know he's planning some daring move."

"Vanity is The Penguin's weakness," said Batman. "It has brought him down more than once." He looked straight at Gordon. "But *cunning* is his strength, Commissioner. It wouldn't be wise to forget it."

"I am well aware of that," Gordon said. "If he wants the Black Egg — and I'm convinced that he does — then he thinks he has a way to get it."

Gordon ran a hand through his hair. "I know what The Penguin is capable of doing, but I have to say he's bitten off more than he can chew this time. Stealing a two-ton statue, four thousand pounds of solid stone? And from right under our noses at that? The Black Egg is guarded night and day by the finest security system in the world. How does he think he's going to pull this off?"

The plaza was nearly empty now. Most of the officers were packing up their gear. Some of the patrol cars pulled away, as the TV crews and newspaper reporters arrived on the scene. Batman could hear them complaining because the patrolmen on duty wouldn't let them past the yellow tape.

"He already *knows* how he plans to do it," Batman told Gordon, remembering his bouts with The Penguin in the past. "He already has a way."

14

Gordon looked down at his feet. "This threat, his boast that he intends to get rid of you. He's dead serious about that, you know."

"I know he is," said Batman. "My *funeral* would please him about as much as getting away with the Black Egg."

Batman rested one hand on Gordon's shoulder. "I don't intend to let that happen, but thanks for your concern." He waved a hand at the black platform. "He's not *through,* you know. It's three days until Halloween. We'll hear from him again. He'll have to put on a show for us, before he goes after the Black Egg."

Commissioner Gordon frowned. "What makes you think he'll wait until Saturday night? He could strike any time before that."

"He could." Batman showed Gordon a dark smile. "But he won't, because he's The Penguin. Whatever else he is, he's an actor, Jim. And an actor *has* to have a big audience to watch him perform."

"*Hmmmph!*" Gordon made a noise in his throat. "We're talking about a criminal act here, Batman, not a big Broadway show!"

"Tell that to The Penguin," Batman said.

The morning sun broke through the low clouds and sliced across the glass face of the Burson Tower. A few weeks before, a man had rented office space on the thirty-fifth floor. The man rented the office under the name of Rodger deRaven, an antique dealer from Paris, France. The man wasn't an antique dealer, and he wasn't from Paris, France. He was a member of the underworld in Gotham City, and

15

once he rented the office, he never came near the Burson Tower again.

A few nights later, workmen wheeled in half a dozen large wooden crates and took them up the freight elevator to the thirty-fifth floor. The crates were labeled "office equipment," but there were no computers, file cabinets, or furniture inside. One of the crates contained two dozen neatly racked umbrellas. Each umbrella was a weapon that could spew out bullets, poison gas, razor-sharp darts, or a deadly sheet of flame. Other crates held up-to-date burglary tools and dangerous explosives.

One crate held the short, pudgy man who now watched the plaza in front of City Hall with powerful German binoculars. Earlier, he had watched the young rookie, Bobby Meaders, as he stumbled upon the black coffin. He had watched the police cars scream onto the scene. And, moments after that, he had seen Batman arrive and hurry to Commissioner Gordon's side.

At the sight of Batman, the pointy-nosed figure drew a deep breath and held it. His fingers tightened around the binoculars. He could hear his own heartbeat and feel the blood racing through his veins. His whole body trembled with rage. A deep, frightening sound rumbled up from his throat, a sound like a wolf who has just caught sight of his prey.

He felt so much hatred for the tall, dark-clad figure in the plaza below that the glass in his binoculars seemed tinted blood-red.

When the coffin exploded, sending a shower of water and black powder over the startled policemen, the man in the

Burson Tower threw back his head and howled. A smirk of delight crossed his features as the officers scurried about for cover. He had to lower the binoculars and wipe the tears of laughter from his eyes.

The Penguin watched from high above until Batman left the scene. He followed the caped figure with murder in his eyes.

"Have a nice day," he said, grinning. "You don't have many *left,* Batman!"

The Penguin crossed the room and sat down in the big easy chair he had hidden in one of his crates. He was satisfied with his work so far. His old enemy knew he was back, and now the real fun could begin.

The storm that swept the city in the early-morning hours had moved quickly off to the west. Only a distant roll of thunder was left to remind The Penguin of the night he had spent in the high tower. He had slept very little. He had dreamed that something terrible and cold, something without a name, had chased him through the nightmare hours before the dawn. . . .

CHAPTER 3

"The Owls Screech Tonight!"

The Batmobile raced through the morning, out of Gotham City. Its motor hummed with power, and the heavy tires whined on the still-wet streets. As the last dark clouds disappeared, the Batmobile approached Wayne Manor. The holographic image of a steep, rocky hillside wavered for an instant, and the sleek machine vanished into the safety of the Batcave.

Batman quickly shed his costume, shaved, and changed into gray trousers and a white sport shirt. Alfred was waiting when the elevator brought Bruce Wayne up to the first level of Wayne Manor.

"I thought you would be arriving quite soon," Alfred said. "Breakfast is ready in the dining room, sir."

"Thank you, Alfred, I'm starved," Wayne said. He followed Alfred through the vast living room and into the dining area.

"I've been watching the TV," Alfred said, as he placed

toast, bacon, and orange juice at Wayne's place. "The news is on all the channels. I see that little monster's back again."

Alfred made a face. "A Halloween funeral. What extremely bad taste, if I may say so, Master Bruce."

"No one ever accused The Penguin of having good taste," Wayne said. He finished his orange juice in one swallow and looked directly at his friend. "He's after the Black Egg of Atlantis. He hasn't *told* us this, of course, but he might as well have announced it on billboards all over Gotham City."

Wayne glanced out the high window at the dark woods of the estate. "The crime itself is pretty obvious, Alfred. But there's more to this business than that."

"Are you speaking of The Penguin's threat on your life, sir?" Alfred asked.

Wayne shook his head. "No. The Penguin *has* to brag. That's nothing new. I'm talking about what *else* he has in mind for Gotham City. He'll try to steal the Black Egg, all right. But that's only part of his plan. He's said it before: 'A perfect crime is a work of art.' He's a ham actor, Alfred. He'll let us know he's around — *before* the big Saturday-night event."

Alfred brought a fresh orange juice. "I think he's gone too far this time," he said. "He has pulled off some amazing robberies before, but stealing the Black Egg of Atlantis, in front of hundreds of people. . . . That's a bit daring even for The Penguin."

"That's exactly what Commissioner Gordon said," Wayne told him. "I don't blame him for thinking it's next to impossible to get past the museum's security. But The Penguin is no ordinary criminal. Selling him short would be a dangerous thing to do."

"There is a great deal of truth in that, sir," Alfred said, recalling The Penguin's crime sprees of the past. More than once, the rotund little genius had pulled off robberies that baffled the police, and almost cost Batman his life. Armed with his trick umbrellas, The Penguin had used his twisted brain to rob the citizens of Gotham City of diamonds, rare paintings — almost anything of value one could imagine, as long as it belonged to someone else. Alfred still wasn't convinced The Penguin could steal the Black Egg — but the wily little crook would make life miserable for everyone while he tried.

After breakfast, Bruce Wayne returned to the Batcave to take another look at The Penguin's habits. Every scrap of information available on the nation's top criminals was stored in the memory banks of Batman's computer. Batman believed these thousands of recorded facts were among his most valuable crime-fighting tools. Even the cleverest of criminals — such as The Penguin and The Joker — made mistakes now and then. Criminals thought they were "different" in every way from honest citizens, but Batman knew this wasn't true. Everyone had certain "patterns" to their life. They liked certain foods, favored certain places, and followed the same habits, over and over again. A person's habits were as revealing as his fingerprints, if you knew how to read them.

Batman knew The Penguin well, and he was certain the

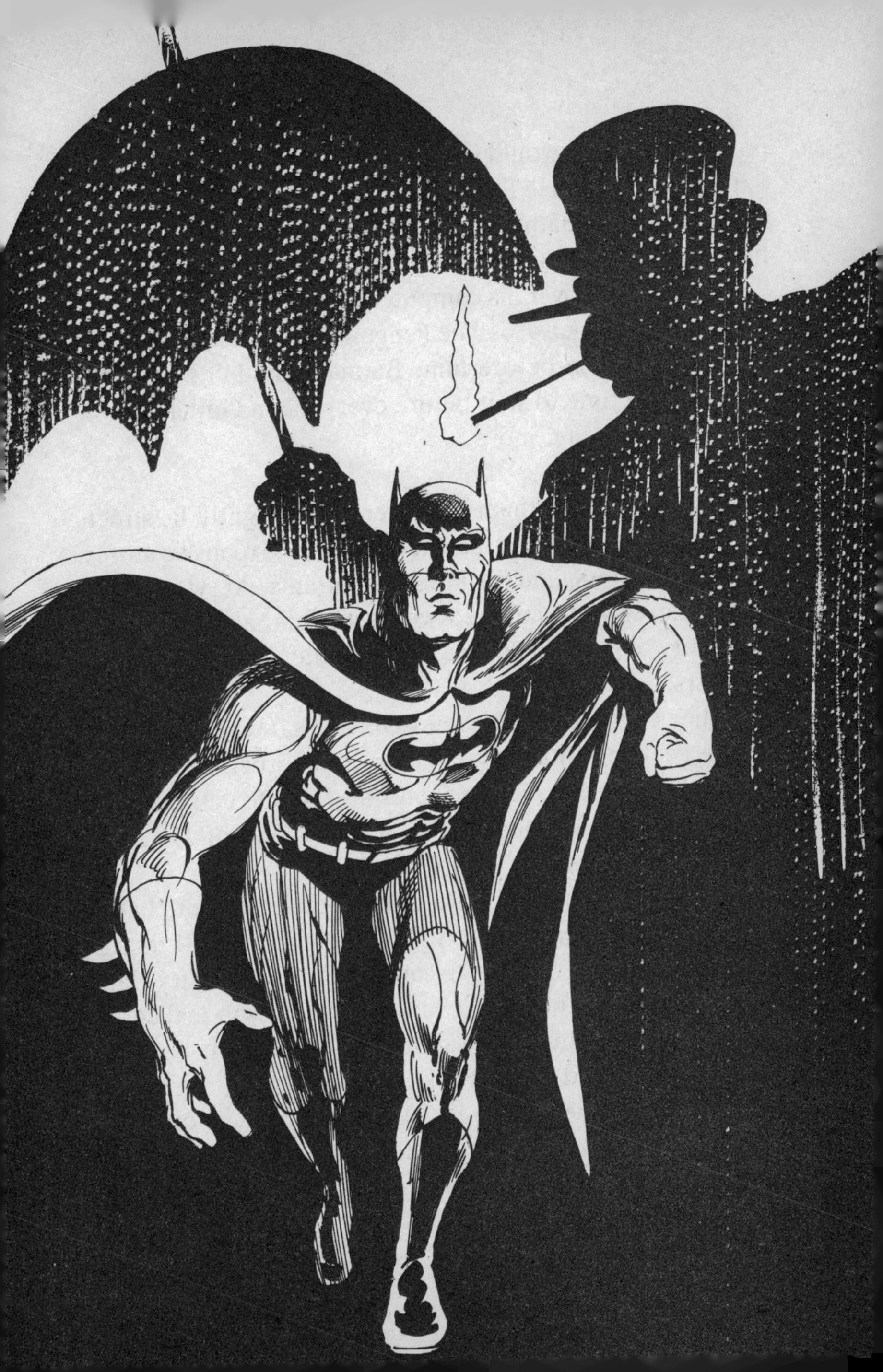

portly crime king would show his presence somehow before Saturday night. "He'll have to let me know that he hasn't lost his touch," Batman said aloud. "Just *where* he'll strike first is the question."

Batman bent over his computer again. His fingers moved rapidly over the keys, as The Penguin's criminal past flashed by on the screen before him. Batman couldn't know that he had little time to wait before everyone in Gotham knew The Penguin's first move. . . .

In the heart of Gotham City were the brightly lit streets and broad avenues that boasted the most expensive stores, the best theaters, and the finest restaurants. At twenty after eight, stores were jammed with shoppers, and there were no empty seats at the Palace or the Rialto, the city's favorite theaters.

Police Commissioner James Gordon sat with lieutenants Rosie Peekner and Pierce Tanaka at a corner table in Delaney's Restaurant. It was Gordon's favorite eating spot in town, and he was looking forward to one of Delaney's famous twelve-ounce T-bone steaks.

"Frankly, I wouldn't have given a nickel for our chances of getting a decent meal tonight," Gordon said. "I thought the TV people were going to camp out forever in City Hall."

"If I ever get my *hands* on the person who leaked that funeral note, they'll be walking the waterfront beat until they retire," said Rosie Peekner.

The tall brunette looked grimly at Commissioner Gordon. "This is just the kind of thing we want to avoid," she said. "I agree with what Batman told you, sir. The Penguin *loves* to see stories about himself in the papers and on TV."

"It is not very hard to get the public worked up over something," Tanaka added. "Not when you have the news people cranking out stories like this."

Tanaka frowned at the open paper on his lap. The headlines screamed in bold black letters:

A FUNERAL FOR BATMAN?
"SATURDAY'S THE NIGHT!"
THE PENGUIN SAYS.

Gordon shook his head. "Well, it's out in the open now. We'll have to deal with it as best we can. It doesn't make our jobs any easier, but we'll handle it somehow."

Commissioner Gordon's face brightened as the waiter set his order down before him.

"Ah," he said with a grin, "now that's more like it. Crime in Gotham City will have to wait while I sink my teeth into this!"

Gordon picked up his knife and fork. The problems of the day seemed almost worth it, now that his reward was there sizzling on his plate.

"What time is it?" Lieutenant Peekner asked. "I think my watch has stopped."

"It's eight-thirty-six," Tanaka said. He smiled at Rosie Peekner. "You have a date or something, Rosie?"

"What I *have* is a watch that doesn't work," Rosie said firmly. "And if I *did* have a date, Pierce Tanaka, it wouldn't be any of your —"

A high-pitched scream cut off Rosie's words. Peekner, Tanaka, and Gordon all turned at once to stare at the back

23

of the restaurant. A woman in a red dress was weaving crazily through the tables, tearing at her hair. A tall, elderly man fell out of his chair, dragging tablecloth, silverware, and a plate of grilled salmon to the floor.

"What on earth —!" Gordon stood quickly, dropped his napkin on the table, and ran in the direction of the trouble, Peekner and Tanaka behind him.

The panic had spread to other tables now. A short man bolted down the aisle and ran headlong into a waiter balancing a large tray of food. The waiter went head over heels, sprawled across a table, and hurled his tray through the air. Five orders of Delaney's special pea soup went flying, splattering clean white shirts and fancy hairdos a brilliant green.

Rosie Peekner grabbed Gordon's arm and pointed toward the door to the kitchen. Gordon looked and spotted the source of the trouble at once. At first, he could hardly believe his eyes. It *couldn't* be, but it was. *Owls!* Dozens of screeching, fiery-eyed, coal-black owls were swarming out of the kitchen like a living tornado. They flapped wildly about the room, veering and slicing through the air, dipping down to nip at faces and tear at people's hair.

Gordon saw a few brave customers had held their ground. They swatted at the creatures with trays and water pitchers, any weapon they could find. One man jabbed at a wild-eyed bird with his fork. The bird screamed and clawed the man's chin.

Most people ran. They howled and shoved each other aside. The owls cut through the air and swept down like angry hornets on the panic-stricken diners.

Gordon tried to stop the mad rush for the doors, and

24

nearly became a casualty himself. The frightened customers bolted past him with fear in their eyes.

Tanaka was suddenly at his side. The officer shouted at him, but Gordon couldn't hear a thing above the noise. Finally, Tanaka gave up, grabbed Gordon's arm, and pushed him toward the front door. Gordon saw Tanaka was right. There was nothing they could do inside. The crowd stampeded all around them, like buffalo before a prairie fire.

"Where's Rosie?" Gordon asked, when he and Tanaka reached the sidewalk outside. "Have you seen her anywhere?"

"Over there," Tanaka said. "She helped a lady out who had two kids. The woman could only handle one."

A man rushed past Gordon, nearly knocking him to the ground. If possible, the scene was even *worse* outside. Horns blared as cars rear-ended one another in the street. Shoppers fled the stores screaming as maddened owls dropped down from the skies. Gordon saw a cloud of dark birds attacking a group of women huddled before the Palace Theater.

Rosie Peekner appeared as sirens began to wail in the distance.

"Help is on the way, sir," she said, rolling her eyes to the sky. "We've got units coming from every precinct in town. All available fire engines and ambulances are rolling right now."

"We're going to *need* those ambulances," Gordon said. "I'm afraid we've got a lot of injuries here." He shook his head in disbelief. "I have never seen anything like this in my life. Can *owls* go *crazy?* If they can, it's a new one on me."

Gordon stopped and looked up at the sky. Thousands of bits of paper were floating to the streets like snow. Rosie picked up one of the leaflets and handed it to Gordon. The commissioner glanced at the paper and made a low, angry sound in his throat.

"It's him," he said darkly. "That pudgy little monster's behind all this, I *knew* it!"

He frowned at the leaflet and read it again:

THREE DAYS TO GO BEFORE THE BIG EVENT —
THE FUNERAL OF BATMAN!

It was signed, of course, by The Penguin.

Gordon crumpled the paper in his fist and tossed it to the ground. The streets were suddenly silent. Gordon looked up again. As quickly as they had come, the owls had disappeared. . . .

CHAPTER 4

"Something Deadly, Something Dark . . ."

It was nearly two in the morning before Batman left Commissioner Gordon's office. The police radio had alerted him to the trouble, and he had hurried to the scene at once. The owls were gone by the time he arrived, but it was easy to see where they had been. Wreckers hauled off cars that had collided during the attack. The red and blue lights of emergency vehicles flashed off the broken windows of stores and restaurants. Ambulances howled into the night. The Penguin's leaflets blanketed the street. TV and newspaper reporters stopped anyone who would stand still long enough to talk.

"You were right," Gordon said. He sank wearily into his chair, and ran a hand through his thinning hair. "The Penguin didn't waste any time."

"I'm afraid this is only Act One," Batman said. "He'll hit us again. Probably harder next time. We were lucky. From your Lieutenant Peekner's reports, it looks as if no one was very badly hurt. A lot of scratches, and a couple of broken arms and legs. It could have been much worse."

Gordon leaned across his desk and clenched his fists. "When I get my hands on that — that long-nosed little runt!" The commissioner sighed and shook his head. "No use getting mad, I suppose. It won't do any good. The best thing we can do right now is try and outguess him. Try to figure out *where* he'll hit next. I've got Tanaka and a couple of his men on the computers right now. They're listing every likely spot in Gotham City where plenty of people gather. They're going over every public event of any size that takes place between now and Saturday night."

Gordon looked at Batman. "It's a pretty hopeless job, I'm afraid. There are *hundreds* of places The Penguin might strike. There is no way on earth I can cover them all."

"All you can do is place officers at the most obvious targets," Batman said. "Maybe we'll get lucky."

"I'm going to pick out the top five Tanaka comes up with," Gordon said. He stood, jammed his hands in his pockets, and stared out the window at the darkened plaza below City Hall. "I also intend to have SWAT teams in roving vans covering different sections of the city. If anything happens, the nearest team can rush to the scene in a matter of minutes."

Batman could see his old friend was nearly out on his feet. He was sure Commissioner Gordon hadn't slept since The Penguin's first "surprise" outside of City Hall.

"You ought to try and take a break while you can," said Batman. "You aren't going to do Gotham City any good if you're walking in your sleep. Have you stopped to eat in the last twelve hours?"

Gordon's eyes blazed. "Don't talk to me about *food,*" he said. "I was just about to cut into the finest-looking steak I've ever seen when that — that umbrella freak let loose his herd of owls!"

"Flock," said Batman.

"What?"

"It's a *flock* of owls. Elephants come in herds, Commissioner. Owls come in flocks."

"Call 'em anything you like," Gordon grumbled. "My *steak* got trampled in Delaney's, and The Penguin's going to pay for that!"

Batman tried to hide his smile. "There's one more thing," he said. "I know we didn't get any ravens or crows from The Penguin's first attack, but Lieutenant Peekner tells me a couple of owls were killed in the Palace Theater."

"So?"

"Why don't you have the boys at the police lab go over those birds," said Batman. "See what they can find."

Gordon gave Batman a curious look. "You've got something in mind, I can tell. You want to let me in on it?"

Batman shook his head. "If I knew what I was looking for, I would. It just seems strange to me that those ravens, crows, and owls would be that vicious. It's not natural for birds to act like that. Most any creature will defend itself if it has to, but *these* birds turned on people, without any reason."

"Hmmmmm." Gordon looked thoughtfully at his hands. "Maybe The Penguin *trained* them to attack. I wouldn't put it past him."

"Maybe," said Batman. "I'm not going to make any guesses until we see what the lab boys find out."

Batman didn't get to bed until well after four in the morning. Still, he was up again at seven, sitting down to breakfast, reading the morning papers Alfred had left at his place. In spite of the few hours' sleep he'd had, he felt rested and ready to go. Batman had trained himself to get the most out of whatever sleep he managed to get. The criminals of Gotham City didn't work from nine to five, and Batman had to be ready to face them at any time.

"The Penguin is certainly getting himself in the news, Master Bruce," Alfred said, setting a cup of hot chocolate on the table. "There is nothing in the papers but news of last night's owl attack. It is all they're talking about on the television, too."

Bruce Wayne picked up his cup and looked out at the bright morning. "I expect he's happy, then, Alfred. There's nothing The Penguin likes better than being the star of the show." He glanced at his watch. "I'd better get moving. I have to be at the Gotham City Mall by ten."

Wayne downed the last of his hot chocolate and stood. He was about to go upstairs when he happened to catch Alfred's eye.

"Now what's that look supposed to mean? And don't tell me it's nothing at all."

"I was just thinking that you ought to be extra careful today, sir," Alfred said. "This ceremony at the mall is a big event. It would be an ideal place for The Penguin to put on one of his disgusting displays."

Wayne smiled. "That crossed my mind, Alfred. There are also two art-show openings, a national business meeting, a music festival, an automobile show — and that's just part of the list. The Penguin can't hit them all."

"I understand that, Master Bruce," Alfred said. "Just keep your eyes open, sir."

"I'll do that," Wayne said. He clapped his old friend on the back. "And thank you for the thought."

After Bruce Wayne left, Alfred cleaned up the breakfast dishes, then fixed himself a cup of tea and two pieces of toast. Usually, he walked through Wayne Manor every morning at this time to make sure everything was in order. On this particular morning, however, he found himself staring out upon the broad green lawn.

Alfred wondered if he should have told Wayne what was really on his mind. He had slept very little the night before. Alfred usually had very pleasant dreams, but last night had been something else again. He had awakened just at dawn after a terrible nightmare. He was alone, running across a black and empty plain. He didn't dare look back. Something dark and deadly was on his heels, he knew that. He also knew that if he turned around and *faced* it, it would swallow him up right there. He could feel its cold breath, cold as a blast of winter air. He could hear the sound of its great leather wings, and smell its damp and sour fur. He could feel its razor beak, snapping and clacking at his back. . . .

And that was the moment Alfred woke up, his body covered with sweat, his heart beating wildly against his chest.

He thought about the nightmare, and decided that he had done the right thing. Master Bruce had enough on his mind without hearing about some silly dream.

Alfred kept himself busy all morning, and tried to put the nightmare aside. Still, no matter how hard he tried, the thing wouldn't go away. . . .

As one of the wealthiest men in Gotham City, Bruce Wayne spent as much time as he could encouraging other well-to-do citizens to contribute to worthy causes and lending his own name to money-making events. Today's affair in the giant Gotham City Mall was a book sale to pay for a new mobile hospital van that would serve the needy citizens of Gotham City. Books of all kinds were on sale, and several famous writers were on hand to sign autographs.

Wayne, as chairman of the event, made a very short speech, urging the mall's shoppers to stop by the sale and telling them their purchases would help a worthy cause. When he moved away from the microphone, a tall, attractive woman with fiery red hair stepped into his path and held out her hand.

"Mr. Wayne?" she said. "We haven't met, but I thought that we should. I'm Dr. Amelia Torn."

Wayne looked at the woman a moment, then remembered. "Of course, *the* Dr. Torn, the woman who discovered the Black Egg of Atlantis. I was hoping to get to meet you before the opening of the museum Saturday night."

Dr. Torn bit her lower lip and nervously rubbed her hands. "That's why I want to talk to you. I read in the paper that you'd be here, and I thought . . . I am *worried* about the opening. All this talk on the TV. . . ." She paused and looked painfully at Wayne. "They're saying that this awful Penguin person might try to steal the Black Egg!"

"If they're saying that, then they are only guessing," Wayne said. He made a mental note to tell Gordon that someone in his department was talking too much. "You can be sure the police and the museum security will be on guard against any kind of trouble."

"I know," said Dr. Torn, gazing out across the mall, "but if there is any *chance* that something might happen, I — I think we ought to call off the opening. I don't see how anyone could get away with a statue that weighs two tons, but if it were *damaged* in any way . . ."

She frowned and shook her head. "I know many famous scientists don't believe the Black Egg came from the lost continent of Atlantis, but they're *wrong,* Mr. Wayne. I *found* it, and I *know* this is one of the biggest discoveries of the century, whether anyone believes it or not!"

Wayne wasn't surprised at the anger in the woman's voice. He had read several articles about Dr. Torn, and knew that she had flown into a rage more than once when someone doubted the importance of her find. He couldn't blame her for that.

"I would hate to see you cancel the opening," Wayne said, "but that's up to you. The Black Egg belongs to you, Dr. Torn. I'm sure the directors will understand if that's what you decide to do."

Dr. Torn raised a brow. "It's *your* museum, Mr. Wayne,"

she said shortly. "I imagine the directors will understand what *you* want them to understand."

"You're wrong, if that's what you think," Wayne said. "The Wayne Foundation funded the museum. The directors run the show over there, and *I* stay out of the way."

Amelia Torn caught the tone of his voice, and decided she had gone too far. The color rose to her face. "I shouldn't have said that, Mr. Wayne. I must apologize. When it comes to the safety of the Black Egg, I don't think straight sometimes."

Dr. Torn looked at Wayne. "May I tell you something, Mr. Wayne? It has . . . bothered me a little that the unveiling of the statue takes place on Halloween. The Black Egg is a *serious* find . . ."

"It's my turn to apologize," Wayne said. "Someone should have explained that to you. The directors felt that since Halloween is a night of mystery, it would be an ideal time to introduce one of the greatest mysteries of our age. The people who will attend this special opening are the same people who support the museum — *and* the future expeditions of people like yourself. They *will* come to this Halloween opening, and I assure you they'll take you seriously, Dr. Torn. I'm certain you'll benefit from this showing."

"Yes . . . yes, I see," said Dr. Torn. She smiled at Wayne. "I'm afraid we scientists get so wrapped up in our work sometimes, we don't think about the—"

A terrible shrieking sound tore through the air. Wayne looked up, startled, as a cloud of dark shapes burst through the glass roof of the mall. Splinters of glass showered down

34

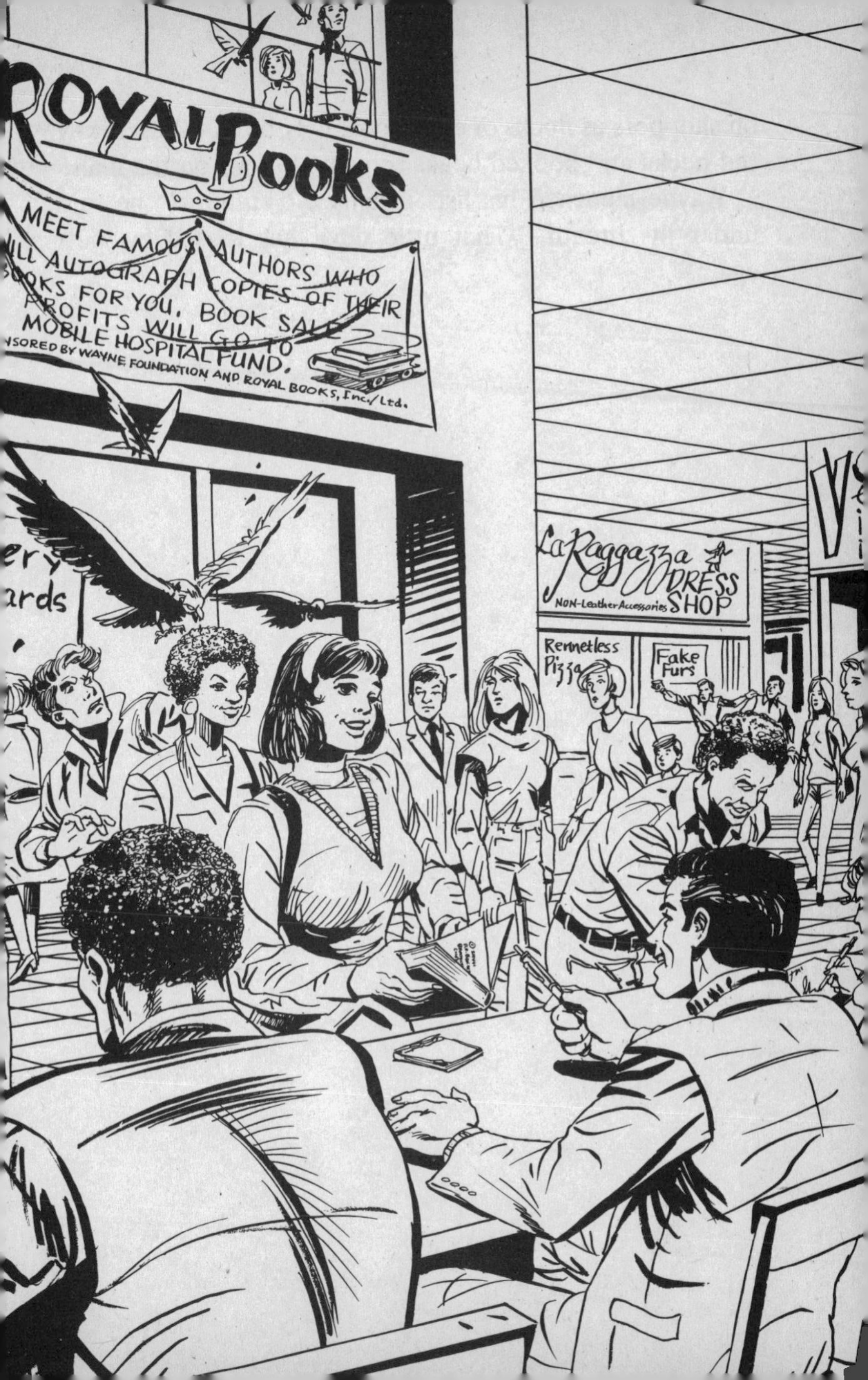
ROYAL Books
MEET FAMOUS AUTHORS WHO
ILL AUTOGRAPH COPIES OF THEIR
OOKS FOR YOU. BOOK SALE
PROFITS WILL GO TO
MOBILE HOSPITAL FUND.
NSORED BY WAYNE FOUNDATION AND ROYAL BOOKS, Inc./Ltd.
ery
ards
LaRaggazza DRESS SHOP
NON-Leather Accessories
Rennetless Pizza
Fake Furs

on shoppers as flocks of enormous, ugly birds with scrawny red necks and hooked beaks screamed down on the mall.

Wayne clenched his fists in anger. "*Vultures!*" he said under his breath. "That little devil has loosed his pets again!"

CHAPTER 5

"You've Outsmarted Yourself This Time, Penguin!"

"Quick, in there!" said Wayne.

Dr. Torn opened her mouth to speak. Before she could finish, Wayne jerked open the door to the pet store directly behind him and pushed Dr. Torn inside.

"Get to the back," he said. "*Stay* there, and don't come out!"

Wayne dodged through the panicked crowds, heading for the entry to the parking garage. The hideous black vultures swooped down from above, flapping their giant wings, and snapping at the frightened shoppers.

Rushing into the vast, multilevel parking garage, Wayne found his green Jaguar, opened the door, and ducked inside. He pressed a button beneath the dash, and the passenger seat slid forward, revealing Batman's cape, hooded cowl, and gloves — his complete crime-fighting costume, carefully packed for a quick change. The car's tinted windows hid his movements, and in less than three minutes Batman was running back toward the mall.

The scene that faced him there made his throat go dry. The mall was filled with screaming black vultures, red-eyed birds with yellow beaks and sharp claws. Hundreds of frightened people ran for cover. Some ducked into stores, while others tried to reach the doorways leading outside. Batman saw that one exit was clogged with shoppers fighting and pushing to get free. They were too scared to think about what they were doing, and many were in danger of being crushed.

A vulture swept down from above, its claws spread wide, going for Batman's face. Batman lowered one shoulder, clenched his gloved fist, and sent the vulture tumbling through the air, dark feathers flying. He thought about using his Batarang, but decided that weapon was useless here. He could bring down a few of the birds, but a few wouldn't help. Besides, the Batarang was a dangerous weapon, and there were too many innocent people around.

Batman swept his gaze around the mall. *Something* . . . he needed something that would work, something that would drive the birds away. . . . He spotted what he needed on a wall across the way. A firehose was coiled there in a rack. He ran quickly to it, jerking the long hose free. A security guard saw Batman and stumbled over to him. A vulture's beak had torn a long red gash along the man's jaw.

"Batman, anything I can do?" the guard asked.

"Turn that wheel and get me some pressure," yelled Batman. "Then grab the hose behind me, and keep it from getting tangled up!"

"Right," said the guard, "you've got it!"

Batman gripped the heavy brass nozzle and ran to the railing that overlooked the level below. Suddenly, he could feel the surge of power in the hose. He flipped the release switch open, and a strong jet of water sprang free. He raised the hose high, and aimed it at a vulture diving on the crowd below. The hard stream of water caught the bird in midair, slamming it to the ground. The security guard cheered. Batman spotted another bird, circling high above. He waited until the vulture arched its wings to dive, then aimed the jet of water in its path. The vulture shrieked in anger, flapped its wet wings, and fell like a rock.

"You've got them on the run," the guard shouted. "Let 'em have it, Batman!"

I don't like to hurt birds, Batman thought to himself, *but I don't see that I have any choice. . . .*

- Working his way along the railing, Batman sent birds reeling right and left, keeping them off the crowds below. The vultures kept coming, but there were only a few left now, and those birds still in the air wanted nothing to do with the fierce stream of water.

From the corner of his eye, Batman saw that the Gotham City police had arrived. They were handling the crowds, getting people safely outside, and caring for those who had been hurt in the attack.

Batman watched the last black bird disappear through the broken glass roof, and turned off his hose. He thanked the guard for his help and took the escalator downstairs. As he walked toward the group of uniformed officers, a familiar voice called out from his right. Batman turned and saw Commissioner Gordon striding quickly down the mall.

39

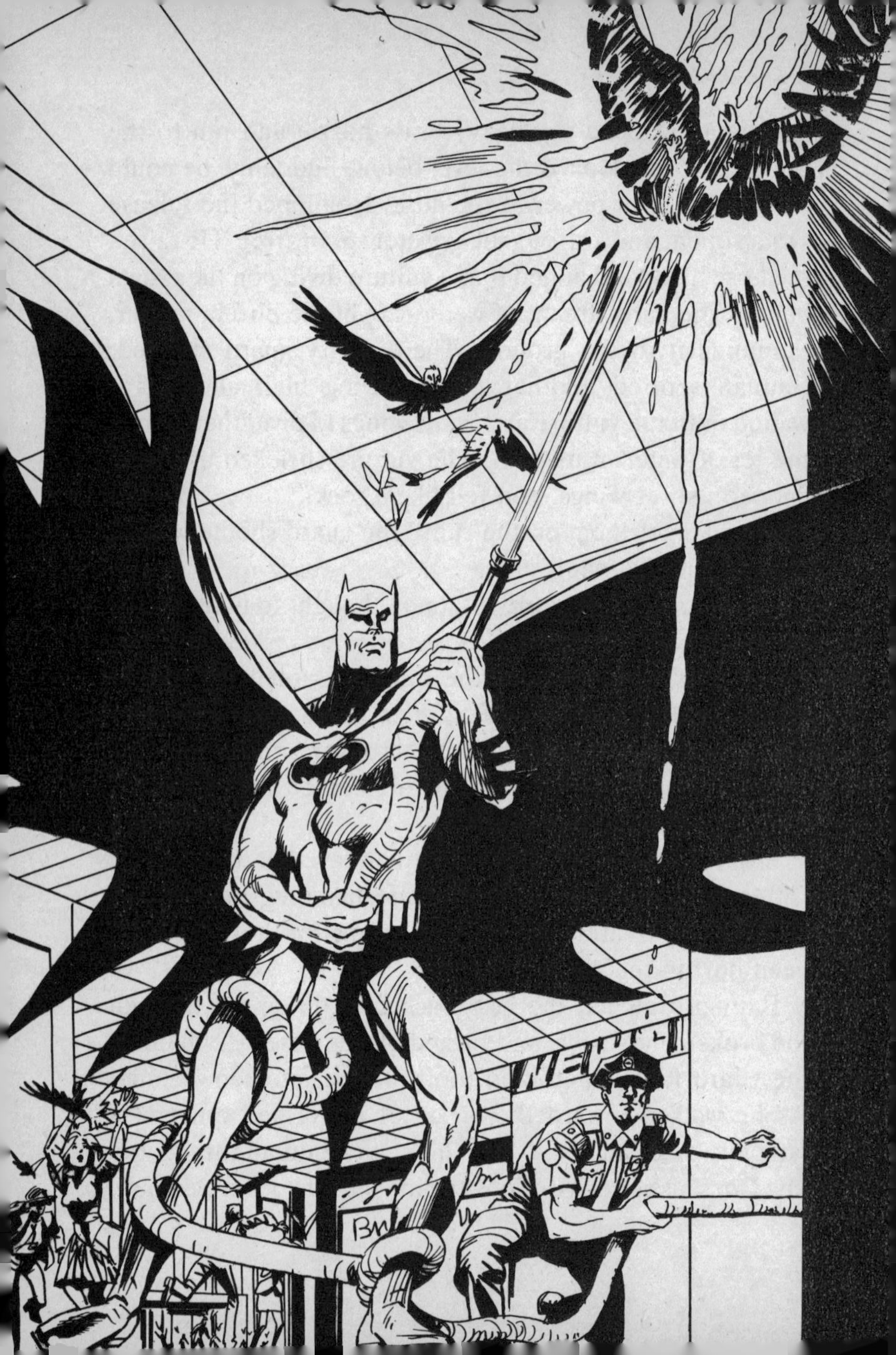

"Well, you got here pretty fast," Gordon said with a look of surprise on his face. "How did you manage that?"

"Just luck, I guess," said Batman. "I was in the neighborhood."

"I'm glad you were." Gordon grasped Batman's hand. He looked around the mall and shook his head. "This place was on my list, but not right at the top. We're covering as many likely targets as we can. *Vultures.*" The commissioner made a face. "And I thought *owls* were bad."

"I don't think there are too many injuries," Batman said. "But one is too many." He looked down the mall at the scattering of broken glass and fallen birds. "Some criminals break into a business or a house when no one is around. That's bad enough, stealing other people's property. But The Penguin goes further than that. He has no respect for human life. That's what makes him so dangerous, Jim. He'll go to any length to get what he wants, and he doesn't care who gets in the way."

"I've got some news for you," Gordon said. He reached into his vest pocket, unfolded a piece of paper, and squinted at it through his thick glasses. "Your hunch was right. The lab boys examined those owls killed in the theater district. They were drugged. I could give you a fancy name for it, but it's easier to tell you what the drug *does*. It drives the birds crazy — turns them into flying killers. You put that stuff in their veins and they're not afraid of *anything*. One tiny drop, and a sparrow will go after a Bengal tiger."

Batman listened, then let out a breath. "I'm not surprised, Commissioner. Birds simply don't act the way these did. There had to be another answer."

"Well, now you've got it," Gordon said, slipping the note back into his pocket. "Though I don't know what good it'll do us in fighting The Penguin."

"It tells us one thing," Batman said. "The Penguin's never cared about people, but he's always had a soft spot for birds. Now, he doesn't care about their well-being either." Batman looked straight at Gordon. "We're dealing with a man who's gone over the edge, Jim — a criminal genius who may be totally mad."

"I'm afraid you're dead right," Gordon said. "He was bad enough before. If we're dealing with a *maniac* now . . . ." The commissioner shook off the thought and nodded toward the mall door. "Lieutenant Peekner and I were headed out to the museum when we got the call about the trouble here. I want to take another look at the security there. I'd like you to come along, if you can."

"I think it's a good idea," Batman said, "but you don't need me for that. Let's get together later on. I'd like to spend some time going over The Penguin's crimes of the past."

"Fine," Gordon said, "maybe we'll get a break, and my men will be on hand next time he pulls something like this."

"Maybe so," said Batman.

Even if you have men there, Batman thought to himself, as he watched Gordon walk toward the exit, *The Penguin will be somewhere else. He'll send his crazed birds out to fight, but he won't show up himself. He's saving his big appearance for Saturday night. . . .*

*   *   *

It was after ten at night, but Batman still crouched over his computer, bringing one image after another to the screen. Hours before, Alfred had brought a sandwich to the Batcave, but Batman had hardly touched it. His eyes began to burn, but he knew he couldn't quit. It was there, somewhere, hidden in the thousands of entries on The Penguin. Batman knew if he could find that single clue, maybe only a word or two, he would learn how The Penguin planned to steal the Black Egg.

Glancing wearily at his watch, Batman saw it was nearly eleven o'clock. He knew he was getting nowhere at all. All The Penguin's clever schemes were right there, but nothing jumped out and said *this* is what the little umbrella fiend will do next.

Batman rubbed his hands across his eyes. *Maybe I'm looking in the wrong place,* he thought. *Maybe it's not The Penguin's past I need to study. Maybe it's —*

Batman came suddenly alert. His fingers moved rapidly over the keys. Bright images flared on the screen. Barely ten minutes later, Batman leaned back in his chair and smiled. He liked what he saw on the screen. And, in his mind, he saw a picture he liked even better — The Penguin, with a number on his shirt, looking at the world through prison bars.

Just before midnight, Alfred came down to the Batcave to urge his old friend to get some sleep. The computer still glowed in the dark, but Batman was gone. . . .

The museum was dark and cool. Standing quietly just inside the security doors, Batman could hear the faint whisper of the heating and air-conditioning system that kept the museum at a steady sixty-eight degrees year-round.

Batman had turned down Commissioner Gordon's invitation to inspect the museum because he knew he would learn nothing new. As Gordon had said, there was no finer security system in the world. Invisible beams of light crisscrossed the floor like phantom spiderwebs. Video spy cameras were mounted on every wall. There were electronic "traps" that could detect a footstep anywhere in the museum.

Anyone but Batman would have set off a dozen alarms by now. But, as Bruce Wayne, he had designed the security system himself. Before he drove onto the museum grounds, he had punched in a signal from the Batmobile that would let him pass freely through the system inside.

Out of the corner of his eye, Batman saw the squat, veiled statue of the Black Egg of Atlantis. It stood on a low platform in the heart of the museum. Even though it was covered now, the sight brought a queasy feeling to the pit of his stomach. He *knew* the Black Egg was only a statue, but he couldn't shake the thought that something dark and evil lay hidden in that ugly piece of stone.

Batman moved like a shadow through the Aztec exhibit, and past the great idols of ancient Egypt. A doorway at the far end of the museum led down to the lower level, where relics were stored for future showings. There, he found the narrow passage that took him down farther still, to the sub-basement of the museum. The walls here smelled musty and damp.

Using his small flash, Batman studied his map. It had to be there, he knew. Maybe a little more to the left . . .

Yes! A smile creased his features. There it was, a rusty manhole cover set in the floor. The museum had been built over the ruins of a building that had stood for more than fifty years in Gotham City. This sub-basement, Batman knew, had been a part of that old building.

Batman found a piece of steel construction rod and used it to pry the manhole cover loose. A cold, stale odor drifted up from the open hole. Batman's flash was nearly lost in the darkness below. Lowering himself down on his Bat-Rope, he slid twenty feet to the stony floor.

Batman smiled again. There it was, just as he had seen it when he sat at his computer in the Batcave. As he'd studied the bright screen, reviewing The Penguin's past crimes, the thought had come to him that he must *think* like The Penguin, do exactly what The Penguin might do: study the target well, and find a way into the museum that no one else would even imagine. Batman had punched in old maps of Gotham City and found the answer staring him in the face. *This* was The Penguin's secret, a long-abandoned branch of Gotham City's earliest subway system, a dark and silent tunnel that ran directly beneath the museum itself.

Batman stared into the blackness. He knew what he would find down here.

"I've got you now," he whispered into the shadows. "You've outsmarted yourself this time, Penguin!"

CHAPTER 6

"Monsters Everywhere!"

It did not take Batman long to discover that he was right. The Penguin *had* been in the tunnel, and not too many days before. The king of tricky umbrellas had tried to cover his tracks but he had left several telltale clues behind. Past an abandoned, rusting subway car, Batman found a powerful hydraulic lift that would allow The Penguin to lower a heavy load from the concrete ceiling above — a load like the Black Egg of Atlantis. Farther back in the tunnel, Batman discovered an old work cart resting on the subway rails.

And on the damp ceiling of the tunnel, he discovered the most important evidence of all. The Penguin had scratched a faint circle on the ceiling. He had tried to smear dirt over the markings, but Batman spotted it. The circle markings told him all he needed to know. The sub-basement and the museum's lower level came to a halt some ten yards to the west. The Penguin would *not* have to bore through these levels — the circle he had drawn was directly beneath the Black Egg itself, on the main floor of the museum. The Penguin would use some powerful cutting tool to break through the concrete ceiling of the tunnel. He would lower the Black Egg to the hydraulic lift, then set it on the railway cart. Batman had studied his maps well, and he knew the abandoned tunnel led right to the waterfront. The Penguin would have a boat waiting, and he would disappear over the dark waters with the Black Egg. First, Batman guessed, he would arrange for a power failure that would plunge the museum — and probably half the city — into darkness.

Batman knew his enemy well. On Saturday night, The Penguin would pull off his daring robbery right under the noses of the police and the hundreds of guests on hand for the unveiling.

"You'll try, won't you?" Batman whispered to the dark. "You'll have to show off, and when you do, I'll be waiting for you. . . ."

Police Commissioner Gordon paced back and forth across his office carpet like a tiger stuck in a cage. His tie hung loose, and his sleeves were rolled halfway up his arms. It was only nine-thirty Friday morning, but he felt as if he had already put in a full day. People were shouting and shaking their fists in the hallway outside his office, demanding to be let in. The phone hadn't stopped ringing since dawn. Everyone from the city dogcatcher to the mayor himself had something to say.

Gordon opened his door and called out to his secretary. "I don't want to see *anyone*," he said. "No one, okay? I don't care if the *President* calls!"

47

He closed the door and leaned against it, scowling at lieutenants Peekner and Tanaka. "This town's gone crazy," he said. "Everyone out there is completely nuts! Gotham City is coming unglued, and *I'm* supposed to stick it back together!"

Lieutenant Pierce Tanaka cleared his throat. "About those reports of, ah, giant snakes in Greely's Department Store on Sixth Avenue, sir? I sent a car over there an hour ago, and there aren't any snakes. At least, there aren't any now."

Gordon stared at Tanaka. "Well, I'm pleased to hear that, Lieutenant. You don't know how *happy* I am to learn that we don't have giant green snakes in our largest department store."

"Pink snakes, sir."

"What?"

"The report said pink snakes, Commissioner."

Gordon showed Tanaka a weary smile. In his job as Police Commissioner of Gotham City, he had learned that sometimes you had to laugh at things that weren't very funny at all. Either that, or go crazy like everyone else.

And *crazy* is the word for Gotham City right now, Gordon thought. Since The Penguin's "bird attacks" had begun, police stations all over town had been flooded with strange reports. People saw peculiar lights in the sky. One man said his canary had given him a nasty look. Another said his Saint Bernard dog had begun to talk. A woman reported monsters were having a picnic on top of her garage.

The newspapers and the TV stations hadn't helped. They "hinted" that the Black Egg of Atlantis might have brought

48

"dark forces" with it from the depths of the sea. When fierce storms had lashed at the city, the newspapers blamed the Black Egg. They said the "hideous statue had used its evil powers to darken the skies."

"Put as many officers on nut calls as you can," Gordon told his lieutenants. "But we have to remember that *real* crimes haven't come to a halt in Gotham City, just because people are seeing spooks everywhere."

Rosie Peekner ran a hand through her dark hair. "It's not getting better out there, sir, it's getting worse. I've told my sergeants that they are *not* to let our officers answer calls unless they feel there is some real danger to human life."

"That should cut out about ninety percent of our false alarms," Lieutenant Tanaka put in. He jammed his hands in his pockets and frowned. "I can't *prove* it, Commissioner, but I have an idea our local criminals are *enjoying* this. I think they're making some of the crank calls, just to tie us up."

"I wouldn't be surprised," Gordon said wearily. "The newspapers, the TV people, the burglars and thieves — everyone's having fun with this mess except us." He shook his head and gazed out the window. "I wonder why I wanted to be a policeman? It seemed like a good idea at the time. . . ."

High above the city in his Burson Tower retreat, The Penguin laughed aloud. It was a high, cackling sound, very much like the call of some rare jungle bird. The Penguin was having the time of his life. He was sprawled out in his

49

easy chair, watching TV. Perched atop a belly the size of a small watermelon was a half-eaten cheeseburger, and the remains of a lemon pie. He was dressed in a starched white shirt and gray pants. His high silk hat and black coat hung on a rack across the room, along with a dozen or so brightly colored umbrellas.

Now and then, The Penguin pressed his handy remote control, switching channels from one news broadcast to the next. What he saw brought a broad grin to his face. Gotham City was in a panic. Everyone was frightened out of their wits. There was even a rumor of a riot at City Hall.

"Hah! Look at *that*," he cried out, "the poor creatures don't know what to do next. They're running around like bugs on a hot stove! Dee-lightful. Absolutely dee-*lightful!*"

"It sure is, boss," Bumper said.

"You've got 'em on the run for sure," Lice chimed in.

Lice and Bumper sat side by side on straight-backed chairs. Each was as tall and skinny as The Penguin was short and fat. They were cousins, but they looked enough alike to be brothers. Both of them had heavy black brows that grew together and sad, droopy eyes. Faded yellow hair hung down across their shoulders like mops someone had left out in the rain.

"*Bumper*," shouted The Penguin, "I feel the need of a pink lemonade. *Lice* — will you do *something* about the color on this set? All the people are *green*. I do *not* like people who are green!"

The instant The Penguin spoke, Lice and Bumper scrambled to their feet. The Penguin liked people to jump. He

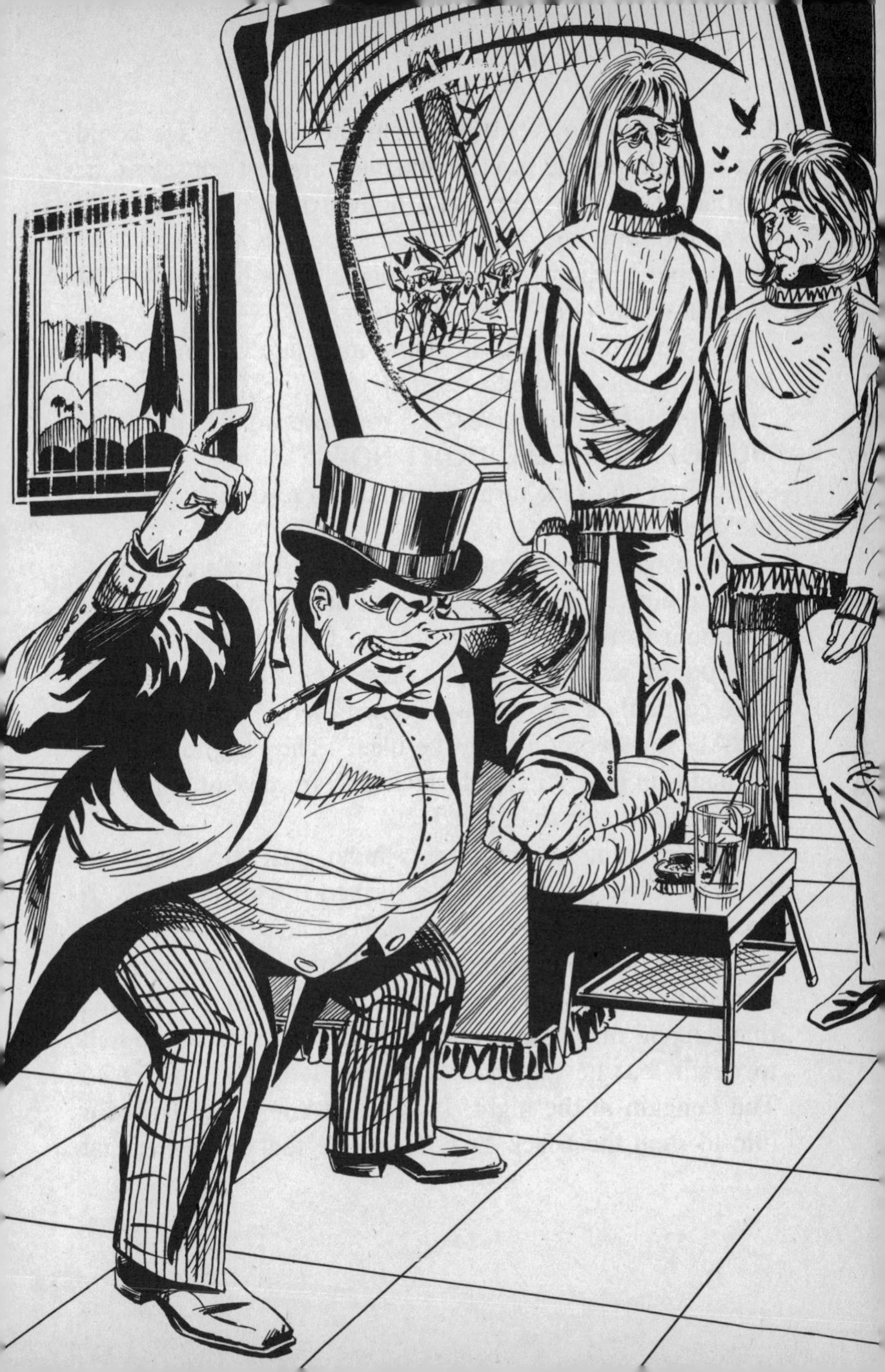

liked them to stay a little nervous all the time. He could not tolerate people who might speak up for themselves, or anyone who would *dare* have a thought of his own. *He* would do all the thinking. All they had to do was *jump*.

Bumper brought a pink lemonade. Lice jiggled the TV knob until the people weren't green.

The Penguin turned on them and glared. "Well, what are you *idiots* standing around here for?" he shouted. "Don't you see what *time* it is? You have work to do. GET OUT OF MY SIGHT RIGHT NOW!"

Bumper and Lice turned pale, then raced each other for the door.

"As usual, I am surrounded by fools," The Penguin muttered to himself. He slid out of his chair and waddled across the room to the window that faced City Hall. Maybe the man on TV was right. Maybe there *would* be a riot. There were certainly a lot of people down there.

"Ah, now wouldn't that be nice!" The Penguin rubbed his hands in glee. "I could watch it all from right here, and that's even better than live TV!"

The Penguin let his gaze wander past the towers of Gotham City. Bright sunlight flashed off his monocle. It was nearly high noon, but The Penguin's dark BB eyes seemed to find something far beyond the daylight, into the dark of night. He was getting used to the dreams. The thing that flapped through his restless hours still scared him half to death, but he understood it now. It had whispered to The Penguin in the night. It had told him it was *right* for him to steal the Black Egg. The force that lay inside that frigid stone had been imprisoned there for thousands of years. Now, The Penguin would set it free. . . .

The Penguin looked up, startled. For a moment, he wasn't exactly sure where he was. Then he remembered: The Black Egg . . . the dark thing that chased him through his dreams.

During his long criminal career, The Penguin had never believed in anything he couldn't steal and hold in his chubby little hands. Now, he wasn't that certain anymore. Was it only a dream, or did some creature really whisper to him in the night?

He turned around quickly, certain that something was there. But there was nothing at all. The Penguin was alone in his room. . . .

Commissioner Gordon wasn't taking any calls. But when the red phone rang on his desk he picked it up at once. It was Lieutenant Peekner, calling from the Gotham City Sports Center. As Gordon listened, the blood rose to his face. He squeezed his right fist and snapped a pencil in two.

The Penguin had struck again. Black petrels, cormorants, ospreys, and snapping gulls had swept down on the international swim meet. The governor, the mayor, and important guests from around the world had been attacked by crazed seabirds. The birds had struck terror among the swimmers and onlookers alike, and several people were hurt. Police and ambulances were rushing to the scene.

This time The Penguin's message read:

One more day before BATMAN dies!

Gordon set the phone back in its cradle. "You pointy-nosed lunatic," he grumbled aloud, "when I get my hands on you I'll — I'll dip you in birdseed and throw you to the pigeons in City Park and see how you like that!"

CHAPTER 7

"Take a Deep Breath, Batman —
It's Going to Be Your Last!"

All day Saturday, heavy polluted clouds hung just above the towers of the city. When the citizens of Gotham could see the sun at all, it looked like a twenty-watt bulb behind a curtain that hadn't been washed in several years. The chill that had gripped the city all through October disappeared. It was humid and hot, and the air was too heavy to breathe. The TV weathermen said they had never seen a Halloween like this. It was more like the Fourth of July than October 31.

"This is all we need," growled Commissioner Gordon, "crazy weather on top of everything else!" He glared at the plaza far below. "If there are any nuts *left* in town who haven't called me on the phone, they will now. We're going to have demons in every closet, and spooks in every tree."

"It's started already," Rosie Peekner said. She glanced at the small black notebook in her hand. "A guy in Marble Heights says a dinosaur's in his backyard. He says it's stomping all over his prize flower bed."

"Rosie, I don't want to *hear* it, okay?" Gordon pressed his hands to the sides of his face and closed his eyes. "If you see Pierce Tanaka anywhere, send him in. I want to make some changes in the museum security plan."

Rosie Peekner left. Commissioner Gordon glanced at his watch. It was 3:26. He didn't think The Penguin would bother with another of his "air raids" today. More than likely, he was saving himself for the big show tonight.

"That rolly-polly waddler has bitten off more than he can chew, this time," Gordon said. "An *army* couldn't get near that statue tonight!"

Gordon believed that he was right. Tanaka and Peekner had done a fine job, and he was certain there was no way The Penguin could cart off four thousand pounds of solid stone. Still, the commissioner had been in police work a long time, and he knew that *nothing* was impossible in the ugly world of crime. Especially when a master thief like The Penguin was on the loose. . . .

By the time Gordon got home from the office, he was ready to fall asleep in his tracks. Instead, he barely had time to take a bath and get ready for the long night ahead. He wasn't too surprised that Batman hadn't called after Friday night's seabird attack. There wasn't much to talk about. As usual, The Penguin had very likely used his hired gangsters to handle the "little jobs." He, himself, would make his grand appearance at the museum.

"He can't do it," Gordon told himself for the hundredth time that day. "*No* one could pull off a caper like this. . . ."

While he mumbled to himself, Police Commissioner James Gordon tied his bow tie wrong four times in a row.

If the citizens of Gotham City were acting a little stranger than usual for Halloween, you couldn't tell it at the opening of the Thomas and Martha Wayne Memorial Museum. The vast main floor was packed with men in tuxedos and women in colorful formal gowns.

Dr. Amelia Torn, wearing a white sequined dress, moved quickly through the crowd and smiled at Bruce Wayne.

"I never got to thank you," she said. "You pushed me into that store, and probably saved my life."

"Oh, I'm sure you would have been all right anyway," Wayne said.

"Well, *I'm* not so sure," Dr. Torn insisted. "I'm very grateful for what you did. Those awful vultures . . ." She paused, then, and looked curiously at Wayne.

"I tried to find you after Batman drove the birds away, but you had just — disappeared somewhere."

"I, ah, there were several people hurt," Wayne said. "At the far end of the mall. I tried to help out where I could."

"Oh." Amelia Torn nodded, but her eyes told Wayne she wasn't sure of him at all.

Time to get out of here, Wayne thought to himself.

"I hope you'll excuse me," he said. "I've got to talk to one of the directors of the museum. There is always some last-minute business to take care of at these things."

"Yes, of course," said Dr. Torn.

She watched him make his way through the crowd. Who

does he remind me of? she wondered. She knew she had a very good eye for faces. After the vultures had been driven away, she had gotten a good look at Batman. She remembered his strong chin, and the dark eyes flashing behind his batlike cowl. Bruce Wayne had a chin like that, and the very same eyes. . . .

Dr. Torn laughed at herself. Multimillionaire Bruce Wayne and *Batman?* She decided she really must be nervous about the opening, to imagine a thing like that.

A dozen people stopped Wayne to shake his hand. He smiled at each one and moved quickly through the crowd. He glanced at his watch. It was 10:46. He *had* to get away. There wasn't another second to waste.

"Oh, Bruce, good to see you," said Commissioner Gordon. Lieutenant Tanaka was by his side. "I wonder if we could talk for a moment. I'm sure our security will work well tonight, but I—"

"Sorry, Commissioner, I *must* make a phone call," Wayne said. "We'll talk later on."

"Well, I guess so," said Gordon. He watched Wayne disappear, and noticed he was carrying a thin briefcase at his side. "That's not like Bruce at all," he told Tanaka. "He's usually so polite."

"He probably has a lot on his mind," Tanaka said.

Bruce Wayne hurried through the door at the rear of the museum, and down the steps to the storage level below. From there, he moved through the narrow passage to the dark sub-basement. Using his flash, he saw it was 10:56.

58

Not a minute too soon. He had hoped to be there earlier, but it had taken too long to get through the crowd.

Snapping open his briefcase, Wayne drew out a black cape and hood, gauntlets, and a tight-fitting black suit with the emblem of a bat on the front. Moments later, it was Batman who removed the ancient manhole cover and peered into the blackness below.

Nothing. But he *knew* The Penguin was there, somewhere in the dark.

Batman had kept his knowledge of The Penguin's plans to himself. He knew Commissioner Gordon wouldn't approve, but he also knew placing dozens of policemen in the subway tunnel would tip off The Penguin at once. Batman couldn't risk that. This was something he had to handle himself.

Without a sound, he lowered himself to the hard surface of the tunnel. For a long moment, he crouched in shadow, waiting, listening for the slightest sound. He could hear faint laughter from the party in the museum directly above. Still, no sound came from the tunnel itself, except the slow drip of water on stone.

Batman slid a pair of night-vision goggles over his eyes. The goggles magnified even the tiniest spark of light. Without the goggles, it was pitch dark in the tunnel. With them, he could see the tunnel walls, the tracks, and the abandoned subway car. Everything came to him in an eerie green glow.

Once again, Batman looked at his watch. Ten minutes after eleven. Upstairs, he knew, the crowd would be starting to wander toward the Black Egg in hopes of getting a place up front. Yet there was no sign of The Penguin, or the gangsters he would have on hand to help. No sign of the tools they would use to cut through the ceiling beneath the Black Egg. Where was the hydraulic lift, the railway cart The Penguin would use to carry the Black Egg away? It wasn't like The Penguin to cut things so close.

The minutes ticked away like hours. Batman didn't move. 11:21 . . . 11:42 . . .

Maybe he isn't totally crazy after all, Batman thought to himself. *Maybe he's decided he can never get away with such a bold and daring plan.* Or maybe he, Batman, had been careless and left some clue that told The Penguin his greatest enemy had found him out.

No, that's not it . . . something's wrong . . . something's terribly wrong here. . . .

Batman felt the muscles tighten in his shoulders. He took a deep breath to slow his breathing down. Some people have a sixth sense that warns them when something isn't right. The Japanese *ninja* had used this "sense" as if it were another pair of eyes or ears. More than once in his crimefighting career, Batman's highly developed senses had warned him in time to save his life. Now, crouching in the darkened tunnel, he felt as if the very air was full of danger.

Something's not right . . . something's not right at all! . . .

A faint metallic sound reached his ears.

Click-click!

Batman jerked up quickly at the sound. A hint of motion caught his eye. He saw the great black shadow dropping down upon him from above, a darkness like a huge open mouth. Batman moved in a blur, knowing he was half a second late. A steel net snapped shut around him, crushing his arms against his sides. The night goggles shattered. Batman snapped his eyes shut to avoid the broken glass.

He struggled against the killing grip, straining to break himself free. *Umbrella . . .* The thought came to him as everything began to grow dark. *Steel . . . umbrella . . . caught like a fish . . . The Penguin!*

As the metal trap tightened, squeezing the last bit of air from his lungs, Batman heard a high-pitched shriek of laughter echo down the dark tunnel. A faint image swam before his eyes. He wondered if this vision was real, or if death already had him in its grasp. He thought he saw the abandoned subway car suddenly break free, and start rolling down the track. He thought he saw The Penguin perched atop the car, laughing and waving good-bye.

And as his senses began to fade, Batman was nearly certain he saw the Black Egg of Atlantis latched securely just below The Penguin's feet. . . .

"Take a deep breath, Batman," a voice called out in the dark, "it's going to be your last!"

The crowd moved in close to the large, veiled idol. The museum director made a short speech and introduced Dr. Amelia Torn. The crowd applauded. Dr. Torn stepped forward and smiled.

"I am grateful to all of you for being here for the first public showing of the Black Egg of Atlantis," she began. "As you know, I discovered the Black Egg in the coastal waters of the —"

Suddenly, every light in the museum went out at once, plunging the building into total darkness.

A man screamed. A woman cried out. Shouts of fear and anger rose from the crowd.

"Peekner! Tanaka! Get some emergency lights in here *fast!*" Commissioner Gordon yelled. "Everybody, don't *panic*. Stay where you are! We'll have the lights back in a minute or so!"

Gordon's words were lost as fear spread quickly through the crowd. The commissioner felt a man stumble against him. A hand reached out and grabbed his arm.

Without warning, the Black Egg of Atlantis suddenly exploded in a flare of green light. The crowd froze. A swarm of black parrots shrieked from the top of the statue and flapped wildly about the room.

Commissioner Gordon stared. He could hardly believe his eyes. "It — it's a *fake*," he cried aloud. "It's not real. *The real Black Egg is gone!*"

Batman dreamed he was drowning . . .

The black, icy waters closed in around him, pulling him down into the deep.

"*Sleep . . . rest . . .*" said a voice from far away. "*Close your eyes and sleep . . .*"

"*NO!*" He fought against the darkness, struggled to keep himself awake. He strained against the tightening mesh, drew a single painful breath.

There, use that handful of air and use it well, he told himself, *don't let yourself go under again!*

Batman's arms were crushed against his sides. He tried

to move his hands. His fingers were nearly numb. There —
in his right hand, a faint hint of feeling . . .

Use it, use it!

Sweat beaded on his brow. He worked his cold fingers
into the top of his utility belt.

Can't . . . can't do it . . .

"Yes . . . I . . . *can!*" he said aloud, gasping for another
breath of air.

Batman's fingers closed around a small metal capsule in
his belt. With all the fading strength he could bring to bear,
he worked the capsule around in his fingers, pointed it at
the bands of steel mesh, and pressed the tiny button at the
capsule's base.

Batman heard a low hum of power, as the pencil-thin
laser beam came to life. He could feel the awful heat, even
through his heavy gloves. Slowly, the laser began to slice
through the strong steel mesh of his trap. He sucked air
into his lungs, tensed every muscle and tendon in his body,
and ripped his way free.

For a moment, Batman leaned against the wet stone wall
of the tunnel, letting the feeling come back into his numb
arms and legs. Then, pushing the pain aside, he rushed
down the dark tracks where The Penguin had disappeared.

His watch was broken, and he wondered how long he
had struggled in the trap. Two minutes, three? More than
that? It seemed like forever, but Batman knew time plays
strange tricks when you are fighting for your life. The Penguin was up there in the dark, moving swiftly away with his
prize, certain that his old enemy was dead.

Batman was sure he knew how The Penguin had tricked

him. It was a bold and clever plan, and Batman had to give him credit for that. The Penguin had guessed Batman would do his homework well and discover the abandoned tunnel. He left all the clues that Batman would need to convince him that he, The Penguin, planned to steal the Black Egg at midnight on Halloween. The railroad utility cart and the hydraulic lift had been easy enough to find. The circle on the ceiling was the cleverest trick of all. The pointy-nosed genius had cut through the ceiling several nights *before* Halloween, lowered the Black Egg to the ground, and hidden it well in the subway car. Then, he had put the circle of stone he'd removed *back* in place and disguised the cut edges to make it appear that he had not yet committed his crime.

He knew *I would count on his vanity,* thought Batman. *He was sure I would expect him to strike on Saturday night — and he was right. He used his own weakness against me. . . .*

As he ran down the tunnel, Batman wondered what kind of clever fake The Penguin had left in place of the real one. He was sure it was something that would startle the guests out of their wits. That was the way The Penguin worked — he had to have the last laugh.

Nearing a curve in the tunnel, Batman stopped and bent low over the rails to listen. *Yes!* He could hear it, now, the rumble of the subway car against the rails — and not too far ahead.

He rushed around the curve in the tunnel, and raced down the tracks. White light exploded in his eyes. Lead whined through the darkness, chunking into rock above his head.

Batman threw himself to the ground, as tracer bullets stitched a path along the rails. He quickly rolled aside, and sprang to his feet again. He knew, now, that The Penguin wasn't alone. He wasn't at all surprised. The umbrella king nearly always left his hired guns to cover his retreat.

Lead ripped through the air again, deadly yellow blossoms in the dark. Batman bent low, watching the muzzle flashes up ahead.

Two of them, he thought, and a grim smile creased his features. *You should have waited until I was close. Now I know exactly how many you are. . . .*

Batman stopped, set one foot against the ground, whipped a Batarang from his belt, and launched it into the dark. The curved weapon shrieked through the air.

A few yards down the track, Bumper hung onto the rear of the subway car with one hand. In the other, he gripped a heavy automatic weapon.

"I think I got him!" he called out to Lice. "I think I got Batman!"

"If anyone got him, *I* did," Lice grumbled. "You couldn't hit your foot with a brick!"

"Is that so?" Bumper yelled. "I'm a better shot than you'll ever —" He stopped, and stared back into the dark. "Wha — what was that?"

"What's what?" Lice asked.

"That sound, like some kind of *whistle* or something."

"I didn't hear any— *WUUUUCK!*"

The Batarang struck Lice solidly in the ribs. He cried out once, dropped his weapon and tumbled to the tracks.

"Lice? What is it, what happened?" Bumper blinked into the dark. "Lice? Lice, you *talk* to me!"

Bumper suddenly knew he was alone. He felt something cold creep up his back and his mouth went dry with fear.

"Don't come any closer," he shouted. "Get away from me!"

Bumper jerked the trigger, firing one wild shot after another into the shadows. He fired until the gun clicked empty, then he threw it at the darkness, and reached for the weapon Lice had dropped.

An iron grip clamped around his wrist. Bumper cried out and tried to pull away. A black mask loomed up before him, a mask with sharply pointed ears.

"*WHAAAAAA!*" A sound of pure terror stuck in Bumper's throat. A mouth behind the mask grinned. "I hope you got paid in advance," Batman whispered in Bumper's ear, "because you're out of *work*, friend!"

Bumper kicked out blindly as Batman's fist glanced off his jaw. He felt himself flying through space. A loud noise was ringing in his ears. He had half a second to wonder how awful it would feel when he finally hit the ground. . . .

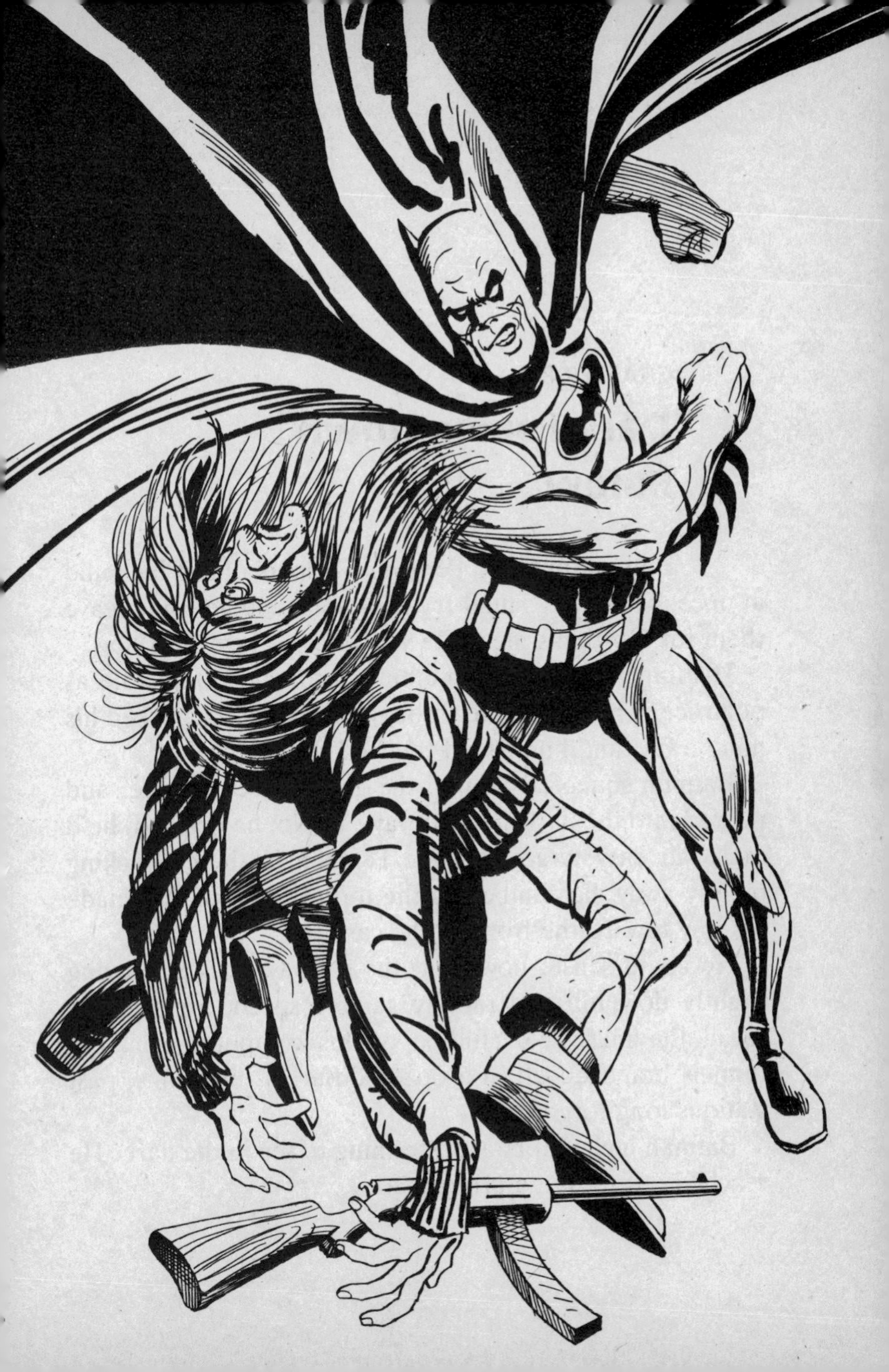

CHAPTER 8

"Dark Forces Down Below . . ."

Batman put The Penguin's helpers out of his mind at once. They were small-fry gangsters, and he could leave them for Gordon's men. He was after a bigger fish now.

His fingers touched something hard, something cold as polar ice. The chill came through his gloves. He jerked his hand away, and knew he'd touched the Black Egg.

Batman squeezed around the great piece of stone, and peered into the darkened subway car. No, he decided, he'd make an easy target for The Penguin in there. Backing quietly away, he climbed to the top of the roof and made his way toward the front of the car.

He could sense, now, that the subway car was moving slightly downhill and rapidly gaining speed. He tried to recall the map he'd studied on his computer. The old tunnels branched off in a dozen different directions, past stations long forgotten.

Batman inched forward, straining to see in the dark. He reached out to find a grip ahead.

Something struck inches from his face. *Chunk-chunk-chunk!* His fingers found a cold shaft half buried in the roof. Another was very close to his neck, and a third blade had pinned his black cloak to the roof. He reached back and jerked the blade free. Another of The Penguin's deadly umbrellas, he thought grimly, one that hurled killing daggers of steel.

A faint sound reached him through the dark. He threw himself quickly aside. Three more razored shafts thunked into the roof — inches from where he'd been only seconds before!

Batman gripped the edge of the roof, slid to his left, and hung from the side of the car. The tunnel wall whipped by, dangerously close. He knew, now, that it wasn't just luck that The Penguin's blades had come so close. The Penguin had *seen* him pressed flat against the roof. And that meant he had night goggles, too — just like the ones the steel mesh had crushed against Batman's face.

He could picture The Penguin up ahead, waiting for his enemy to appear in the weird green light. The moment Batman stuck his head above the edge of the car . . .

"I know you're there," The Penguin suddenly shouted. "No use trying to hide from me, Batman!"

The Penguin laughed, a terrible sound that set Batman's nerves on edge. It was the laugh of a madman, and Batman was more certain than ever that the master of crime had gone over the edge for good.

He inched his feet carefully along a window of the car, moving slowly forward, listening for any sound. The wind screamed by his face as the subway car hurtled faster and faster through the blackness, rocking from side to side.

Risking a look, he peered over the top of the car. Orange fire spat from another of The Penguin's umbrellas. Splinters stung Batman's face. The Penguin laughed and fired again. Batman tensed his shoulders, kicked out hard, and swung himself back to the top of the car.

The Penguin hadn't expected that — Batman had brought himself right into the line of fire. Before he could squeeze off another burst of lead, Batman rolled, leapt into the air, and sprang over The Penguin's head.

The Penguin cried out in alarm. He turned on his heels and lashed out with his weapon at Batman's legs. Batman jumped back, lost his balance for a second, and nearly went over the edge.

The Penguin howled with glee and squeezed the trigger of his trick umbrella. At nearly point-blank range, the bullets tore a fiery groove along Batman's upper arm. The Penguin fired again, but this time his weapon clicked empty. Batman went for him at once. The Penguin whipped his umbrella past Batman's head. Batman ducked and threw a hard right at The Penguin's jaw. The Penguin hopped aside, moving quickly on his short, stubby legs.

The two old enemies faced each other atop the speeding subway car. The Penguin's face was twisted in anger, his eyes bright with rage.

"You had to wait, didn't you?" Batman said. "You could have taken the Black Egg out of here days ago, but then you wouldn't have had me there to see it, would you? You had to finish your act before an audience, Penguin. You

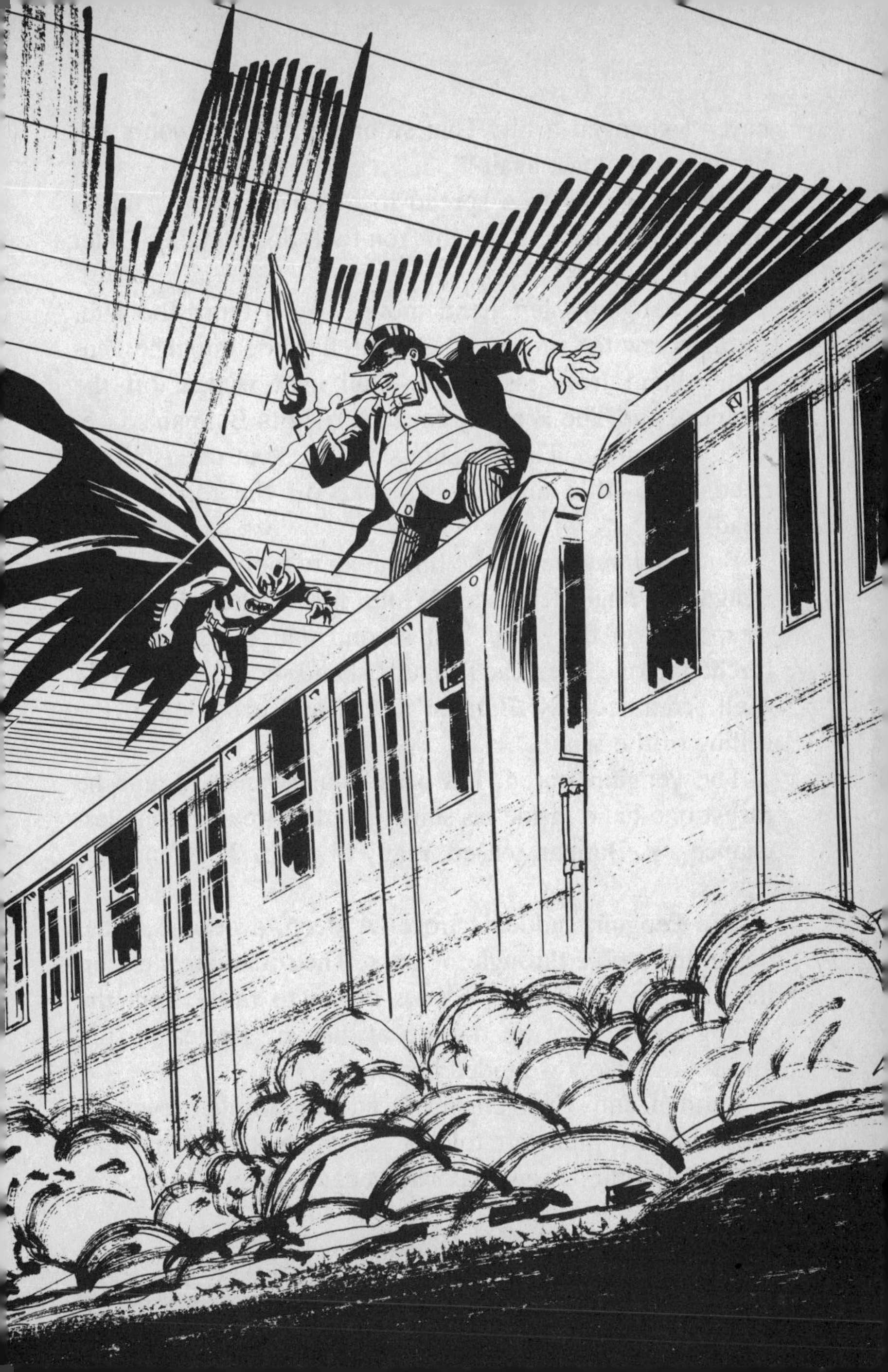

haven't changed a bit. That stubborn pride of yours has brought you down again!"

The Penguin's face spread in a terrible grin. "Who's brought *who* down, Batman? You fool, do you think I'd let you stop me now!"

The Penguin's left hand moved like a blur. Too late, Batman saw the tiny chrome umbrella slide into The Penguin's hand from his sleeve. Dull light winked off the weapon, and The Penguin aimed it right in Batman's face.

"One bullet," The Penguin shouted, "but one is all I'll need. *This* little number will take off the top of your head!"

Batman knew he had no time at all to move. He saw The Penguin's finger tighten. White fire flashed from the weapon — in the same split second that the subway car lurched to one side. The Penguin's hand shook. The deadly shell screamed past Batman's head and exploded in the ceiling of the tunnel.

The Penguin stared. His broad smile vanished, and he thrust one hand inside his shirt. One last weapon, one last chance . . . Batman tensed, ready to go for The Penguin's legs.

The Penguin suddenly froze. A deep, awesome sound began to rumble through the dark. The sound grew closer, like a giant tidal wave. Stones began to rattle from the ceiling and bounce off the top of the car. The earth split and roared like a wounded beast.

Batman and The Penguin faced one another, two old foes with no time left to fight. Batman knew what had happened, and he saw that The Penguin knew it, too. The gunfire had shaken the ancient stone walls of the tunnel, and The Penguin's final shot had done the trick.

Batman turned and ran for the rear of the car, pumping his arms and legs with every ounce of strength he had. He didn't look back. He thought he heard The Penguin cry out, but every sound was lost in the terrible roar as the tunnel gave way and tons of earth and stone came rolling in. . . .

"I'm glad you're safe and sound," Commissioner Gordon said. "But I have to tell you, Batman, I am not at all pleased that you kept this all to yourself. If you had let me know what you found down there . . ."

Batman shook his head. He glanced out the window of Gordon's office. The night was cool and still — the finest sight he'd ever seen. For a moment, as he'd raced down the tunnel ahead of an avalanche of stone, he was sure that he'd never see such a night again.

"It had to be that way, Commissioner," he said. "I had no right to put anyone else at risk."

Gordon muttered something to himself. He had a lot more to say, but there was no use arguing now.

"We've lost the Black Egg of Atlantis forever," he said. "It's buried under so much stone we could never get it out. And just between us, I'm not too sorry that it's gone. Maybe now everyone will stop finding spooks beneath their beds." He gave Batman a curious look. "Imagination can play funny tricks on people. All that talk just about had *me* believing there were . . . dark forces hanging around, something that shouldn't be here at all."

Gordon shook his thoughts aside. "At least The Penguin's gone for good. A pretty terrible way to go, but he brought it on himself. I'm not going to miss the little monster."

Before Gordon could look away, Batman caught the look in his eyes. He read Gordon's thoughts, and understood. Sometimes, you get to know an enemy as well as you do a friend.

"You're right," he said aloud. "I don't guess anyone will be sorry The Penguin's gone."

It was nearly four in the morning when Batman left Commissioner Gordon's office. The Batmobile was in shadow, at the back of City Hall. Batman walked swiftly toward his car, then came to a sudden stop. A fat raven was perched on the hood. It looked right at him with blood-red eyes, spread its broad wings, and vanished into the dark.

For a long moment, Batman didn't move. Finally, he walked to his car and drove toward Wayne Manor through the quickly fading night.

"He's alive," he said softly to himself. "He's out there somewhere mad as a loon and still alive. . . ."

A chill spread over Gotham City. The leaves rattled like bones in the streets. At the Gotham City Zoo, the creatures in the birdhouse grew restless and began to stir about. First one, and then the next, until the entire birdhouse was alive with angry cries. A dove pecked savagely at its mate. A grackle squawked and ripped at a starling, bringing blood.

The sleepy attendant stalked to the birdhouse and shined

his light inside. The birds went silent. A hundred yellow eyes reflected the keeper's light.

Far beneath the earth, directly below the birdhouse itself, a rusted subway car lay buried under tons of crushing stone. Resting on the rear of the car was a squat black figure with a single cold eye. Once before, it had lain in the darkness for four thousand years. Maybe it would sleep that long again. . . .

Neal Barrett, Jr., has written thirty-eight novels and numerous short stories, novelettes, and scripts for comic books. His work spans the field from science fiction, Westerns, historical novels, and young adult novels to mainstream fiction and mystery/suspense.